RULERS AND THEIR TIMES

HATSHEPSUT
and Ancient Egypt

by Miriam Greenblatt

BENCHMARK BOOKS

MARSHALL CAVENDISH
NEW YORK

ACKNOWLEDGMENT

With thanks to J. Brett McClain, doctoral candidate in the
Department of Near Eastern Languages and Civilizations,
University of Chicago, for his most helpful assistance.

Benchmark Books
Marshall Cavendish Corporation
99 White Plains Road
Tarrytown, New York 10591

Library of Congress Cataloging-in-Publication Data
Greenblatt, Miriam.
Hatshepsut and Ancient Egypt / by Miriam Greenblatt.
p. cm.—(Rulers and their times)
Summary: Describes the tumultuous reign of Hatshepsut, daughter of
Thothmes I, and life in ancient Egypt during her reign.
ISBN 0-7614-0911-4
1. Egypt—Social life and customs—to 332 B.C.—Juvenile
literature. 2. Egypt—History—Eighteenth dynasty, ca. 1570–1320
B.C.—Juvenile literature. 3. Hatshepsut, Queen of Egypt—Juvenile
literature. [1. Hatshepsut, Queen of Egypt. 2. Egypt—Social life
and customs—To 332 B.C.] I. Title. II. Series.
DT61.G73 1999 932′.01—dc21   98–21798   CIP   AC

Printed in Hong Kong
1   3   5   6   4   2

Photoresearch by Linda Sykes Picture Research, Hilton Head, SC
Front cover: courtesy of Erich Lessing/Art Resource.
Page 58:British Museum/AKG; pages 6, 10, 14, 20, 22, 31, 53, 60, 65, 73: Erich Lessing/Art Resource;
pages 15, 17, 27, 44, 46, 47, 50: Giraudon/Art Resource; pages 11, 37: British Museum/Bridgeman Art
Library; page 55: Royal Albert Memorial Museum, Exeter/Bridgeman Art Library; page 34, 41, 56: British
Museum; page 71: Egyptian Museum/e.t.Archive; page 5: The Metropolitan Museum of Art/ Fletcher
Fund, 1923; page 48: Royal Museum of Art and History, Brussels; pages 29, 33: Giraudon/Superstock;
pages 38–39: Andre Gallant/The Image Bank.

Contents

The Woman
Who Would Be King

The civilization of ancient Egypt goes back more than five thousand years, to about 3100 B.C.E.* From its beginnings until the fourth century B.C.E., it was ruled by a king, who came to be known as the pharaoh. The people looked upon the pharaoh as a god, a son of the sun god Re. The pharaoh owned the land of Egypt and all it produced. He issued the nation's laws. He was its highest judge, as well as commander in chief of the army. He was also the chief priest.

Some pharaohs were great warriors. Others were famous for the magnificent temples and monuments they built. Hatshepsut was famous for a different reason: she was the first successful female pharaoh to sit on Egypt's throne. Yet for more than three thousand years after her death, no one knew anything about her or her accomplishrnents. It was as if she had never existed.

In this book, you will read about how Hatshepsut became a pharaoh and why the records of her reign were wiped out until just recently. You will learn about how her people lived—the clothes they wore and the foods they ate; their homes, jobs, and amusements; and the way they buried their dead. Finally, you will

*Many systems of dating have been used by different cultures throughout history. This series of books uses B.C.E. (Before Common Era) and C.E. (Common Era) instead of B.C. (Before Christ) and A.D. (Anno Domini) out of respect for the diversity of the world's peoples.

read some letters, poems, and stories in which the ancient Egyptians themselves tell us about their achievements and their dreams.

Hatshepsut was the first great female ruler in history. Her crown and false beard show that the ancient Egyptians considered her their god-king.

PART ONE

Egypt's For

The Nile River was Egypt's Main Street, with boats serving the same purpose automobiles do in the United States.

gotten Ruler

Early Days

Hatshepsut did not care much for war. But no one dreamed she felt that way. Everyone else at the royal court thought war was splendid, especially since the Egyptians usually won.

A long period of warfare had started about fifty-five years before Hatshepsut was born. At that time, in the mid-1500s B.C.E., Egypt was ruled by foreigners known as the Hyksos. They had gained control of most of the country two centuries earlier. Although the Hyksos had adopted Egypt's writing system and many of its customs and religious beliefs, they had never been fully accepted by the Egyptian people.

Nevertheless, the Egyptians at first did not rebel against the foreign rulers—and for a very good reason. The Hyksos had brought out of Asia two terrifying weapons the Egyptians had never seen before. One was a horse-drawn chariot that sped more swiftly than the Egyptians could run. The other was a double-curved bow that shot farther and sank deeper than the simple bow the Egyptians used.

Gradually, however, the Egyptians learned the use of horse-drawn chariots. They also learned how to handle the double-curved bow. Then the cry of "Hyksos, go home!" echoed through the Nile River valley as several local princes raised the banner of revolt.

The first major military campaign against the Hyksos was led by Sekenenre the Brave, prince of Thebes. According to one tale, the campaign began when Sekenenre received a message from the Hyksos ruler Apopi. Although Apopi's capital city lay 365 miles north of Thebes, he claimed he was bothered by hippopotamuses bellowing in Sekenenre's pool. "The pool of the hippopotami, which is in Thebes, must be done away with. For they permit me no sleep, day and night; and the noise of them is in my ears!"

If Apopi was trying to pick a fight, he got more than he bargained for. Sekenenre raised an army of Thebans and led them northward against the Hyksos. His first battles were apparently all victories. But after several years of warfare, he was killed, his skull split by an enemy ax.

Following Sekenenre's death, the struggle against the Hyksos was continued by the prince's two sons, Kamose and Ahmose. Kamose died, perhaps in battle, but Ahmose eventually triumphed and mounted the throne of an independent Egypt.

Ahmose was not content, however, with achieving independence. He wanted to avenge the shame of foreign rule. So he began a series of wars, first to crush Hyksos power in Asia, then to extend Egypt's own frontiers. By the time Hatshepsut was born, her father, Tuthmosis I, ruled an empire that extended "from the Horns of the Earth to the Marshes of Asia"—that is, from the land of Kush (now Sudan) in northeastern Africa all the way to the Euphrates River in present-day Syria.

In many ways, it was exciting for Hatshepsut to have a warrior king for a father. She loved watching the great triumphs, when stacks of loot and thousands of war prisoners bound for slavery were paraded through Thebes. The city's streets were filled with

A statue of Hatshepsut's father, Tuthmosis I. He was the first pharaoh to be buried in a rock tomb hidden in the Valley of the Kings, west of Thebes. Most earlier pharaohs were buried inside a pyramid.

sun-bronzed officers boasting about how many hands they had taken. (Soldiers in those days used to cut off an enemy's hand as proof of having killed him in battle.) Women and children would listen wide-eyed to stories about strange lands where water fell often from the sky and rivers flowed south instead of north the way the Nile did. Each year Tuthmosis I added dozens of gold bracelets and necklaces to his beautiful daughter's jewelry collection. And each year he continued work on the temple complex at Karnak to thank the sun god Amen-Re for giving victory to the Egyptians.

Yet the excitement was mixed with hurt for Hatshepsut. No sooner did Tuthmosis I come back from a military campaign than it seemed that he was off again for another seven or eight months. Of course, it was a king's duty to guard the country's borders. But

Tuthmosis I was doing more than that, and Hatshepsut did not see why. Wasn't Egypt the greatest and most respected nation on earth? Weren't other nations always sending rich gifts to Tuthmosis I in order to stay on friendly terms with him? It must mean that the pharaoh loved fighting more than he loved his only child.

Actually, Tuthmosis I had several children. But the others were the offspring of minor wives and mistresses. Only Hatshepsut had been born to the pharaoh's Great Royal Wife, Queen Ahmose. Nevertheless, Hatshepsut could not look forward to ruling in her own right. It seemed that, according to custom, she would simply marry the male heir to the throne and become the queen consort.

A pharaoh's wives were usually either Egyptian noblewomen or foreign princesses from countries with which Egypt wanted to have close diplomatic ties.

A Talent for Ruling

When Hatshepsut was fifteen, she married a half brother, a royal prince, son of one of the pharaoh's mistresses. He was also named Tuthmosis. He was a sickly youth, and the marriage may or may not have been a love match. But it *was* a success, for it produced a daughter, named Neferure. That meant the Theban ruling dynasty would continue in power.

A few years after the marriage, Tuthmosis I died, and Hatshepsut's husband ascended the throne as Tuthmosis II. Three years later, he, too, died and history repeated itself. The throne passed to the pharaoh's son by a mistress. Like his father before him, the new ruler, Tuthmosis III, had been wed to his royal half sister— Hatshepsut's daughter, Neferure—to make his position more secure. But since Tuthmosis III was only about five years old when his father died, his mother-in-law was appointed regent, to rule for him until he came of age.

Over the next few years, Hatshepsut performed the traditional duties of a pharaoh. She sent out two military expeditions—one south into Kush (sometimes called Nubia), the other east into Palestine—to show that she would maintain Egypt's borders. She held conferences with government officials and decided policy. She dictated letters to provincial governors telling them how much they should collect in taxes that year. She divided the gifts sent by foreign rulers—so much for the throne, so much for the priests of Amen-Re. She read dispatches from Egyptian ambassadors to foreign lands and sent instructions back to them. And she participated in daily religious observances.

Then, after Hatshepsut was regent for about seven years, the political situation apparently changed and a bombshell exploded. Hatshepsut dressed herself in the clothes of a man, put on the false beard that pharaohs traditionally wore, and proclaimed herself king of Egypt!

Hatshepsut received help from several advisers. Probably the most important was the brilliant and powerful Senenmut. In this stone portrait, Senenmut holds Hatshepsut's daughter, Neferure.

It was an extraordinary event, and Hatshepsut must have been an extraordinary person to be accepted as pharaoh in a male-dominated society. She was, however, helped by several extremely able advisers, each of whom represented one or more powerful groups in the country. Hapuseneb headed both the government bureaucracy and the priesthood of Amen-Re. Ineni, a famous architect, had been one of her father's favorite officials. And Neshi was chief of the treasury.

Most important of all was Senenmut. Although apparently a commoner, he was cultured, highly intelligent, and very talented. He eventually held eighty different titles, including those of Steward of the Estates of Amen, Overseer of All Royal Works, and Tutor to the Royal Heiress Neferure. He is best known, however, as the architect of Hatshepsut's mortuary temple at Deir-el-Bahri.

Like most Egyptian tombs, Hatshepsut's mortuary temple stood on the west bank of the Nile. (Egyptians believed the west was the home of the dead because that was where the sun disappeared each night.) When the inhabitants of Thebes looked across the river, they could see the temple's wide terraces rising from the valley floor against the background of a limestone cliff. Hundreds of pale yellow columns gleamed in the brilliant sunlight. Above the terraces were rooms cut into the cliff and dedicated to Amen-Re. Sphinxes—statues with a lion's body to symbolize royal power—lined the road from the riverbank to the temple.

Perhaps the most spectacular part of Deir-el-Bahri was its garden. It contained something that apparently had never been seen in Egypt before Hatshepsut's reign: myrrh trees. Myrrh trees grew in the land of Punt (probably present-day Somalia, on the east coast of Africa). Egyptians used the amber-colored sap from the trees in medicines and perfumes. More importantly, they burned the dried sap as incense before the altars of their gods.

The two hundred statues and relief carvings in Hatshepsut's mortuary temple tell about her supposed divine birth and also describe the voyage to Punt.

The Voyage to Punt

Bringing thirty-one myrrh trees from Punt to Egypt was an important political move for Hatshepsut. For one thing, it probably made her more popular than ever with the Amen-Re priesthood. Punt was supposedly Amen-Re's homeland, from which he left each morning to sail across the sky in his sacred boat and to which he returned at night by way of the Nile that flowed beneath the earth. What better way to please the great god than by making it possible for him to smell his favorite scent as he passed over Egypt?

The expedition to Punt also dramatized Hatshepsut's foreign policy of emphasizing trade rather than conquest. Punt produced many things the luxury-loving nobles of Egypt wanted: gold and ivory, ebony and lapis lazuli, leopard skins and monkeys, to name just a few. In the past, these treasures had been traded from one tribe to another across a thousand miles of grassland and desert before reaching Egypt. Hatshepsut's expedition eliminated the middleman and set up a direct trading route by sea. It showed that merchants could bring back just as much wealth as warriors.

Hatshepsut was so proud of the expedition, in fact, that she had the story carved on her temple's walls. There one can see the five ships that sailed from Thebes, with thirty sailors at the oars of each ship. There is the Puntite village, its round grass huts perched on stilts. There is the village chief, longhaired and bearded. And there is his wife, a very fat lady with a very small donkey to carry

Theban soldiers accompany the trading expedition to the land of Punt.

her everywhere. Trade goods, including the precious myrrh trees, are exchanged. A farewell banquet is held, and at last sails are hoisted for the long voyage home.

At one time, historians believed that Hatshepsut's ships sailed north from Thebes and through a navigable canal that connected the Nile with the Gulf of Suez. According to more recent research, however, this canal did not exist at the time Hatshepsut ruled. Instead, after sailing north, the Egyptians probably unloaded the ships and trekked across the desert to a port on the Red Sea. There they reloaded the goods and sailed south along the coast until they came to Punt. They reversed the procedure for the return trip.

Whichever way they went, the expedition was a tremendous accomplishment. The Egyptians had no maps or records to guide them, nor did they know in advance how many miles away Punt lay. No wonder the inhabitants of Thebes cheered themselves hoarse when the men came back from the farthest known place in the world. The parade through the streets of the capital was probably the most exciting event of Hatshepsut's reign.

Aftermath

Hatshepsut ruled as pharaoh for about fifteen years. After the success of the voyage to Punt, she organized other trading expeditions, to Africa, Asia, and islands in the Mediterranean Sea, including Crete. She obtained wood from Phoenicia with which to build ships for Egypt's navy. She expanded the Sinai copper and turquoise mines and encouraged local manufacturing. She undertook a vast public works program, restoring temples that had fallen into decay and filling Egypt with hundreds of shrines, monuments, and statues. The two obelisks she dedicated to Amen-Re were particularly noteworthy. Each consisted of a single piece of red granite nearly one hundred feet tall (about the height of a twelve-story building) and weighing 700,000 pounds. The pyramid-shaped top was covered with gold that reflected the sun's rays for miles around. For each obelisk, the royal treasurer measured out six bushels of gold—and had plenty to spare. Egypt under Hatshepsut was a wealthy as well as a peaceful land.

Hatshepsut died when she was in her early fifties. She was succeeded by Tuthmosis III, who adopted a very different foreign policy from that of his late mother-in-law. He made fighting "his life's work" and became the greatest warrior and conqueror Egypt ever produced. He led no fewer than seventeen aggressive campaigns into Asia.

But Tuthmosis III did more than that. About twenty years into his reign, he tried to deny that Hatshepsut had ever been pharaoh. He had her name hacked off her monuments. Her statues were dragged from their pedestals, smashed into pieces, and tossed onto rubbish heaps. Only a few small, hidden images of Hatshepsut avoided destruction.

Why did Tuthmosis III do this? Historians do not really know.

One of the few statues of Hatshepsut to survive the fury of her successor

Perhaps he wanted to strengthen his own son's succession by preventing claims to the throne by any of Hatshepsut's relatives. Perhaps he was afraid that Hatshepsut's rule might set a precedent and change the traditional Egyptian view that a woman could be a regent but not a pharaoh. Perhaps it was simply "wounded male pride" that a warrior king had spent part of his reign in a woman's shadow.

For more than 3,300 years, no one knew anything about Hatshepsut. Her name had been erased everywhere. It did not even appear in the list of pharaohs, the dates of her reign being assigned to Tuthmosis III. A landslide covered her lovely temple at Deir-el-Bahri with sand and rubble. Only beginning in the late 1800s C.E. were archaeologists able to piece her statues back together, trace her name underneath the overlying carvings, and re-create the life of the energetic, strong-willed, yet peaceable woman who had once been a mighty king.

Everyday Life in

Farmers winnowed wheat by tossing it into the air so that the wind blew the chaff, or husks, away from the grain.

Hatshepsut's Egypt

"Gift of the Nile"

Although Hatshepsut's empire stretched from northeastern Africa through the Middle East, most Egyptians lived in the valley of the Nile. The valley was shaped like a broom, with a wide triangular top and a long narrow handle, except that the handle was curved instead of straight. The handle was about 12 miles wide. The top, or the delta, was about 100 miles long and measured 135 miles at its widest point. The Nile River flowed northward down the middle of the handle. When it reached the delta, it split, first into two main branches and then into several dozen smaller ones, all of them emptying into the Mediterranean Sea. Beyond the Nile valley, east and west, lay miles and miles of desert.

The Nile originated in the lake country of central Africa, where it was known as the White Nile. About two thousand miles from its source, it was joined by a second river, known as the Blue Nile. The Blue Nile originated in the highlands of eastern Africa, and each year it poured vast amounts of spring rains and melting snow into the White Nile. The resulting flood swept down the valley into the Mediterranean Sea. For as long as the Egyptians could remember, the Nile had never failed to flood each year.

This annual flooding made life possible for the Egyptians. Egypt was indeed the "Gift of the Nile." The river filled wells with drinking water and kitchens with fish. It provided a means of moving people and goods from one end of the country to the other. Most important of all, it enabled the Egyptians to grow food.

Ancient
EGYPT
in the Time of
HATSHEPSUT

The Black Land

The Red Land

0   50   100   150 Miles

0   100   200 Kilometers

CRETE

Mediterranean Sea

Euphrates River

S Y R I A
(Naharin)

PHOENICIA

PALESTINE

Gulf of Suez

Nile Delta

L O W E R

Memphis

E G Y P T

Sinai Peninsula

Nile River

Thebes • Karnak
Deir-el-Bahri

U P P E R

E G Y P T

Red Sea

K U S H

Nile River

© Oxford Cartographers

Farming

Most Egyptians were farmers, and the rhythm of their lives followed the rhythm of the Nile. In November, when the river lay peacefully in its bed, the farmers scattered seeds of wheat on top of the soil. Then they churned the fields with ox-drawn plows to drive the seeds into the ground. Sometimes they let their pigs and sheep into the fields so the animals' hooves would push the seeds still farther into the ground.

The wheat grew rapidly in the hot sun, and the farmers harvested from March through June. The men cut the tassels off the stalks. The women gathered the grain from the ground and put it into sacks, which were then taken to a granary on donkey-back.

During the rest of the year, little or no agricultural work was possible. July through October was the inundation period, when the Nile slowly covered the fields and then drained back into its bed. Yet without the annual flood, there would have been no farming at all. As the Nile receded, it left behind a layer of rich black mud. The mud replaced the minerals that had been used by the previous year's crop. Thus the land was always fertile.

This rich black mud explains why ancient Egypt was often called the Black Land. The name contrasted with the Red Land, the desert that stretched for hundreds of miles east and west of the river.

Because farmers could not work in the fields while the Nile was in flood, Hatshepsut—like other rulers throughout Egyptian history—used the inundation period for construction purposes.

She drafted the farmers and put them to work building temples, digging new irrigation canals, and returning the boundary stones displaced by the river to their proper positions. As payment for their labor, the farmers received food, firewood, cooking oil, and occasionally clothing. Money had not yet been invented.

From sowing seeds to harvesting the crop to carrying the sheaves of wheat away, this mural (*from bottom right to top left*) shows farmers at work in ancient Egypt.

Food

The ancient Egyptians lived mostly on bread and beer. Both were made from grain. A woman would grind the grain between two stones and add water to make dough. Then she would knead the dough, shape it into loaves, and set them aside to rise. If she was making bread, she would bake the loaves in a hearth or a clay stove. (The Egyptians used dung or straw for fuel.) If she was making beer, she would break the loaves into tiny pieces, mix the crumbs with water to form a mash, and let the mixture sit until it fermented. The lumpy beer was then strained. Every village had its corner tavern, and even schoolboys drank two jars of beer a day.

The ancient Egyptians also ate lots of vegetables, mostly peas, beans, cucumbers, lettuce, garlic, onions, radishes, and leeks. Favorite fruits included dates, figs, raisins, and grapes. Fish was popular among the poor. Meat and poultry were usually reserved for the rich. Every wealthy estate boasted a herd of oxen. During the inundation period, the animals were either penned in stalls and hand-fed or were moved north to the delta for grazing. Herdsmen traveling with the cattle kept track of each owner's herd by means of a mark that they branded on the animals' backs with a hot iron. Most estates also raised ducks and geese. In addition, there was a wildfowling industry in marshy areas, where bird catchers trapped the birds in nets.

Rich Egyptians enjoyed wine, particularly white wine. Some-

Workers harvest grapes for making wine. Grape vines had to be watered frequently in Egypt's hot climate.

times, to add sweetness, they mixed the wine with honey or date juice. Sugar was unknown.

All Egyptians—rich as well as poor—ate with their fingers, washing their hands when the meal was over. They also washed every morning and evening. They washed with a natural substance, a soda called natron, and then rubbed oil on themselves to keep their skin from drying out.

Professions and Trades

Girls in ancient Egypt were not allowed to enter professions or most trades. They *could* become weavers, or singers and dancers in a temple. And once in a while, they became traveling musicians, playing instruments such as the flute, the harp, and the one-stringed mandola. But in general—except for Hatshepsut—woman's place was in the home.

Boys, on the other hand, were expected to follow in their fathers' footsteps. The son of a farmer became a farmer. The son of a carpenter learned from his father how to cut down trees with an ax, how to smooth the top of a table with an adze, and how to glue several layers of wood together to make plywood.

There were boatbuilders, blacksmiths, glassmakers, leather-workers, and potters in ancient Egypt. Barbers went from house to house, carrying a razor and a wooden block on which the customer sat while being shaved. Embalmers salted corpses and wrapped them in linen bandages for burial. Sculptors and painters worked mostly on palaces, temples, and tombs.

Another important trade was that of papermaker. The Egyptians had invented papyrus, a kind of paper, about one thousand years before Hatshepsut's reign. They made it from the stem of the papyrus plant, a fifteen-foot-tall reed that grew in the Nile. The papermaker would cut the papyrus stalk into strips. He would lay the strips side by side, overlapping them slightly, and place another layer of strips on top at right angles to the first layer. Then he would wet the sheet, hammer it flat with a wooden mallet, smooth out rough spots with a piece of ivory or shell, and set the sheet in the sun to dry. Books were produced by gluing the sheets into rolls that measured 6 to 17 inches in width and up to 135 feet in length. The Egyptians tied the rolls with papyrus string and stored them either upright in jars, like umbrellas in a stand, or on shelves in a temple.

Egyptians who became soldiers went through a tough period

Workers ply their trades. In the row above, metalworkers melt an ore to separate out the metal and then cool it in water. Below, brickworkers mix chopped straw with clay, soak the mixture for several days, then shape the material into bricks, which are then dried in the sun.

of basic training on joining the army. They made forced marches through the desert and learned how to shoot a bow, throw a lance, and parry sword thrusts with a leather shield. The best soldiers usually became charioteers. War chariots (like the private chariots of the rich) had a wickerwork body open at the back and were pulled by a two-horse team. Each chariot carried two soldiers, one to drive, the other to fight. Unlike foot soldiers, who were bare chested, charioteers wore coats of leather or quilted linen to protect them from attack. But they had problems just the same. A satire of the period tells how a charioteer lost control of his horses and wrecked his vehicle in a ditch just as the commanding general was inspecting the troops. The luckless man was sentenced to one hundred lashes with a whip!

What most Egyptian parents dreamed their sons might become, however, was a scribe. For one thing, a scribe's working conditions were the very best. A weaver got backaches and leg cramps from bending over his loom. A fisherman had to worry about losing his toes to a crocodile. A metalworker "stank more than fish roe." And it was easy to tell a mason by his muddy feet and clay-tainted clothes. In contrast, a scribe's white linen was always spotless, while his office was sprinkled with water several times a day so he would not suffer from the heat.

Then, too, a scribe never had to worry about being unemployed. Few Egyptians knew how to read and write. So jobs for scribes were always available in government service, temples, or nobles' households. Scribes kept all of Egypt's financial records, including the tax payments of cattle and grain. They summarized court cases and made copies of Hatshepsut's decrees to be distributed to her officials. They wrote inscriptions for sculptors to chisel

Pupils learning to be scribes wrote not only on papyrus but also on fragments of pottery or limestone called *ostraca*.

on the walls of temples and monuments. If they were especially talented, they became architects or engineers. And if they wanted to be their own boss, they became freelancers, writing business letters for merchants or magic charms for farmers to place before the statue of a god.

In Hatshepsut's time, there were two forms of Egyptian writing, the hieroglyphic and the hieratic. The hieroglyphic form was written in picture signs called hieroglyphs. Some of them represented words, while others represented syllables or letters. Hieroglyphic writing was used in inscriptions and religious books. The hieratic form of Egyptian looked something like present-day shorthand and was used for everyday correspondence. It was usually written from right to left (like Arabic and Hebrew). Hieroglyphs could be written either way. Both forms were written without vowels. Scribes had to memorize at least six hundred hieroglyphs and an equal number of hieratic signs. No wonder they were honored and respected!

A scribe's equipment consisted of a wooden palette with two cakes of dry ink, a leather pouch for water, and a wooden container for pens. The ink—a mixture of lampblack and gum that the Egyptians had invented about one thousand years earlier—came in two colors, red and black. Writing was done in black. Red was used as a sort of underlining to set off especially important items. The ten-inch pens were made from reeds, and scribes often carried spare ones tucked behind their ears.

This house belonged to an important scribe. It was built on a platform that kept it above flood level.

"Houses of Life"

Egyptian boys learned how to read and write in temple schools—often called the "Houses of Life"—which they attended between the ages of six and twelve. During this time, they usually lived in dormitories, going home only for holidays or other special events. Most students were the sons of nobles and scribes. But sometimes an ambitious, well-to-do craftsman also sent his son to school. That way, the boy had a chance to rise above his father's station.

The school day began early and ended at noon, because of the hot climate. About half the school day was devoted to making word lists or copying page after page from a book of "instructions." These were proverbs, bits of political advice, and rules of etiquette that had been collected and written down over the centuries. "Keep thy tongue from unkind words." "Don't accept the gift of a powerful man." "Wait quietly until your turn comes. . . . [O]ne attains nothing with the elbow." Students were expected to learn how to behave as well as how to write.

The rest of the school day was spent mainly studying mathematics. The ancient Egyptians had symbols for the number 1 and for the powers of 10, but not for the numbers 2 to 9. Thus they wrote the figure 12 as 10 plus 1 plus 1, and the figure 232 as 100 plus 100 plus 10 plus 10 plus 10 plus 1 plus 1. Needless to say, multiplication and division were clumsy operations. On the other hand, the Egyptians developed a good working knowledge of geometry, which they used in surveying land and in building palaces, temples, and tombs.

Discipline in Egyptian schools was strict. It was standard practice for a teacher to hit a boy if he made a mistake in copying or came late to class. As a popular saying put it, "The ear of a lad happens to be on his back. He listens when he is beaten." Between the discipline and the tediousness of learning hieroglyphs and hieratic signs, it must have been a great relief to the students that school let out at noon!

It took students many years to memorize the necessary hieroglyphs and hieratic signs.

The Egyptian Home

Egypt's earliest farmhouses were made of reeds plastered with mud. By Hatshepsut's reign, however, farmers were living in houses made of adobe, or sunbaked mud bricks. The typical house consisted of a single room where the entire family slept,

ate, and worked. Furnishings were sparse. The average farmhouse contained a clay oven, a stand for pots, perhaps a few stone stools, and a handful of woven sleeping mats, which were tossed on the earthen floor at night and picked up during the day.

In the cities, tradespeople lived in larger adobe houses, about fifteen feet wide and thirty feet long. Their four rooms included an entrance hall that doubled as a workroom, a living room, a bedroom, and a kitchen. People often climbed a stairway to sleep on the flat roof, especially during the hot summer. A second stairway led to a tiny storage cave in the ground. Workers in each trade

Egyptian villages today, like those of Hatshepsut's time, are separated from the Nile by a strip of fertile land.

lived along the same street, and their houses shared common walls on either side.

Both city and country houses had high windows for privacy. The windows were either small or covered by gratings. They let in air and kept the strong sunlight out. Additional protection against the heat came from the thick adobe walls, which were sometimes twenty inches deep.

Neither city streets nor country lanes were paved in ancient Egypt. The dust rose in a thin haze. Flies and gnats flew everywhere. And the air was filled with the smells of burning dung, decaying refuse, and fish drying in the sun.

Wealthy Egyptians had more space, and better air. A typical upper-class house was surrounded by palm trees, a grape arbor, a rectangular pool dotted with water lilies, and neat rows of vegetables and flowers, all enclosed within a high wall. The house itself might measure one hundred feet square. It was built on a brick platform four feet above ground level. This kept out scorpions and snakes. (Pet cats helped keep out rats.)

To enter the house, people walked up a ramp and into an entrance hall that contained two rows of wooden pillars, which supported the roof. The hall opened into a large central room. The pillars here were taller than those in the hall, making part of the roof higher than the rest. All the pillars were painted to resemble trees, with reddish brown trunks and bright green tops. The plaster ceiling was painted blue. Sometimes it was sprinkled with gold stars.

Along one end of the room stood a raised platform covered with rugs and cushions, where family members talked and ate. Nearby, a smaller platform held water jars and pots of perfumed salve. Dinner guests used to put the salve on their heads and let it melt. The delicious scent apparently made up for the yellow stain the salve left on the hair.

Behind the central room were the family bedrooms, dressing rooms, and baths. Sleeping on a bed instead of the floor was a status symbol in ancient Egypt. Beds had wooden frames and "springs" of woven cord or leather. Pads of folded linen were placed on top of the springs, and linen sheets were placed on top of that. The pillow was a wooden headrest with a curved support for the neck; it was much cooler than a feather pillow would have been. Since rooms had no cupboards or closets, the ancient Egyp-

The legs on beds and chairs meant for royalty were often carved as lions' paws. The legs on ordinary people's furniture were decorated with grooves.

tians kept their linens, clothing, and toilet articles in brightly painted chests.

The large house also had space for an office, storage rooms, workshops, and servants' quarters. An interior ramp led to the flat roof. The kitchen was in a separate building so the smells of cooking and garbage would not disturb the family.

To light their houses, Egyptians used lamps made of salt that had been soaked in castor oil. A floating wick inside the lamp burned for several hours. To tell time, the ancient Egyptians used a sundial by day and a water clock at night. Sunlight falling on the sundial's pointer cast a shadow that moved around the dial, which was marked with the twelve hours of day. The water clock was a container with a tiny hole near the bottom. Lines inside the container marked off the twelve hours of night. The Egyptians filled the container with water, which slowly trickled out through the hole. The falling water level showed what time it was.

Private Lives

Ancient Egyptians led a close family life. Girls usually married around the age of twelve, boys around the age of fifteen. Apparently, marriages were arranged, but a father almost always took his children's feelings into account. A husband was advised to "love your wife . . . feed her belly, clothe her back . . . [and] gladden her heart." Husbands often gave their wives private names, such as First Favorite, This Is My Queen, or She Is Healthy. Infidelity was frowned upon, and either party could get a divorce if the marriage did not work out.

Ancient Egyptians generally had up to six or seven children. Girls were as welcome as boys. Popular names included His Father Lives, Riches Come, Welcome to You, Chief of the Soldiers, and Ruler of Her Father. Sometimes the name was the first thing said when the baby was born: Ursu ("He's a big fellow!") or, less happily, Kison ("Another brother!"). Sometimes the name praised a god—"Thoth Is Powerful"—or the reigning pharaoh—"Long Live Khephren." Unfortunately, the death rate for children was high. About one-third to one-half never reached their fourth birthday.

Ancient Egyptians often shared their homes with pets. The most popular were geese, monkeys, and cats. Cats were especially popular and were of two kinds. One was a long-faced, big-eared variety with a reddish brown coat tipped with black. The other was a sandy brown variety with black tufts on its ears. The Egyptians associated cats with Bastet, a goddess of motherhood. In at least one city, a person who killed a cat was subject to death by stoning. And it's been said that when a pet cat died of disease or old age, the members of the household would shave their eyebrows and tear their clothes to show their sorrow.

Egyptian weddings were neither legal acts nor religious ceremonies but rather social occasions that included feasting, singing, and story-telling.

Clothing and Cosmetics

Until the age of four, rich and poor children alike ran around naked. After four, boys wore a linen loincloth while girls wore a linen tunic whose hem went up and down depending on the fashion. Members of the upper class covered the loincloth or tunic with a linen robe, accordion pleated and often as thin as gauze. Linen was a very practical fabric. It was strong, easily washed, and cool to wear in the hot climate.

Linen came in just one color: white. The ancient Egyptians added color to their clothing by means of jewelry. The most popular ornament was a flexible collar made of rows of different-colored beads. It was at least three inches deep and sometimes covered the wearer's body from the throat halfway to the waist. The ancient Egyptians were also fond of bracelets and wore them around the upper arms and ankles as well as the wrists. Some jewelry served a double purpose. If it was carved with the eye of the god Horus, it not only looked nice but also was thought to prevent illness and keep off the evil eye.

Egyptian men took great pride in being clean-shaven. Because of the hot climate, many men also shaved their heads. Others wore their hair cropped short but were careful to keep it neatly combed and oiled at all times. They also paid a great deal of attention to its color. The minute a few gray hairs appeared, they rushed to a doctor to try to restore the natural black shade. Oil mixed with the blood of a black ox was highly recommended. If that did not work, the men dyed their hair red with henna. Another concern was baldness. For this, doctors recommended a mixture of six kinds of fat: cat, crocodile, hippopotamus, ibex, lion, and snake. Another "sure cure" for baldness was a mash

Most Egyptians usually went barefoot. Upper-class Egyptians wore sandals made of leather or woven papyrus.

made from date pits, the toes of a dog, and the hoof of a donkey.
On holidays and other important occasions, both men and
women wore elaborate black wigs with long braids or rows of
overlapping curls. The wigs were made either from sheep's wool
or from human hair.

While Egyptian men devoted many hours to the care of their hair, Egyptian women did the same for their makeup. Eye makeup was the most important. A woman began by tweezing her eyebrows. Then she drew an almond-shaped ring of green paint around each eye and put more paint on her eyelids. The paint was made from a copper ore called malachite. It was a germ killer as well as a cosmetic, and Egyptians still use it today to keep away flies and to prevent eye diseases.

Next, a woman brushed red paste on her lips and cheeks and tinted her nails. She also reddened her palms and the soles of her feet. Finally, she took a pill to sweeten her breath and dabbed some perfume on her skin.

Women in ancient Egypt used an eyeliner called kohl to make their eyes more dramatic.

Fun and Games

The ancient Egyptians were a fun-loving people. Children had all kinds of toys: dolls, leather balls and jumping jacks, wooden tops, and miniature crocodiles that opened and shut their jaws when a string was pulled. Young boys spent hours swimming, wrestling, and playing tug-of-war and leapfrog; their sisters enjoyed dancing and juggling. Grown-ups were very fond of board games, especially those played with dice.

The favorite sport of the upper class was hunting. Only nobles were allowed to use a curved throwing stick (something like a boomerang) when fowling. Hour after hour, they sat patiently on boats in the marshes waiting for ducks to come within range. The dead birds were retrieved by specially trained cats. If a hunter was more ambitious, he took a chariot, a bow and arrows, and a pack of greyhounds into the desert to hunt lions, gazelles, and spotted hyenas.

Rich Egyptians also used chariots for racing. As with antique cars today, nothing was too good for these vehicles. Their wheels were painted in brilliant colors. Their reins were decorated with metal ornaments, embroidery, and fringe. And the horses were matched in color and height.

What rich Egyptians liked best, however, was throwing a dinner party. Then the house was filled with excitement. Special rugs and wall hangings were taken out of storage chests and placed in the

The popular game of *senet* was played on a board made of bone, clay, stone, or wood. The pieces of the opposing sides differed either in shape or in size.

large central room. A few carved, inlaid chairs were set up for the most important guests. (Everyone else sat on the floor.) Servants bustled to and fro, arranging piles of fresh fruits and newly baked cakes. A big ox roasted slowly on a spit. Maids wove garlands of lotus blossoms for guests to wear around their necks. Wine jars, marked with the vintage year, were set in metal stands. It was considered rude not to get drunk.

As the guests ate, musicians played and sang. Sometimes the guests clapped their hands in time to the music. Female acrobats and dancers performed at intervals in the flickering torchlight. Perhaps a storyteller recited one of the traditional tales about dwarfs, or magicians, or sailors who had amazing adventures in far-off lands. After everyone had eaten and drunk their fill, the evening was brought to a close with the "Song of the Harper."

> Spend a happy day. Rejoice in the sweetest perfumes.
> Adorn the neck and arms of your wife with lotus flowers
> and keep your loved one seated always at your side. Call
> no halt to music and the dance, but bid all care begone.
> Spare a thought for nothing but pleasure; for soon your
> turn will come to journey to the land of silence.

Life after Death

The ancient Egyptians believed that when they died, they went to the Underworld, where they lived forever the way they had lived in Egypt. Before entering the Underworld, however, they had to undergo several tests.

The first test consisted of avoiding the evil monsters that lurked along the path. The way to do so was by reciting magic spells from a special book, called *The Book of the Dead*. People used to memorize these spells by shouting them over and over at the top of their lungs, hoping the noise would help them remember the words after death.

The second test was a trial before Osiris, lord of the Underworld. The jury consisted of forty-two gods and goddesses, and the soul of the dead person had to swear that he or she had not committed forty-two sins in life. "I have not committed evil against men, I have not mistreated cattle. . . . I have not made anyone sick, I have not made anyone weep, I have not killed." Next, the soul had to swear that she or he had performed good deeds in life, giving "bread to the hungry, water to the thirsty, clothing to the naked, and a lift to the man who was marooned."

Finally, the soul's heart was weighed against the feather of truth by Anubis, the god of embalming. If the heart and the feather weighed the same, it meant the person had been righteous in life. Anubis reported the verdict to Thoth, the god of wisdom and of scribes, who wrote it down. Then the soul was led to Osiris, who welcomed it into the Underworld. However, if the heart weighed more than the feather, it meant the person had been wicked in life, and the soul was thrown to Ammit, the swallower of souls.

Anubis, the god of embalming, was pictured with the head of a jackal. Here, a priest wearing the mask of Anubis performs a ceremony over a mummy.

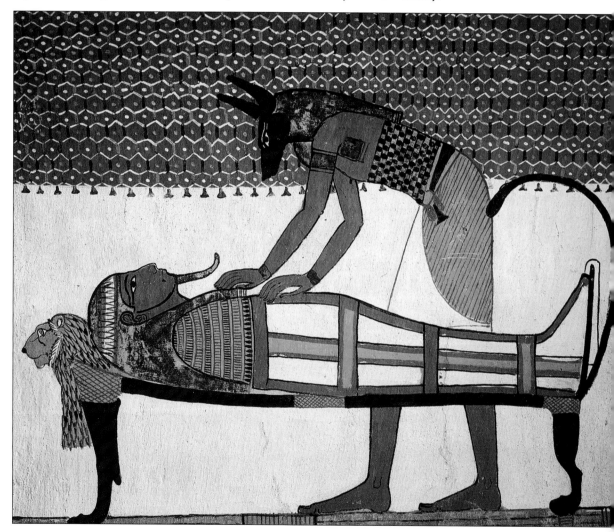

Making a Mummy

Avoiding monsters and being weighed against the feather of truth were not the only difficulties that confronted an Egyptian's soul after death. The soul also needed a body in which to rest for eternity.

At first the Egyptians preserved the bodies of the dead by salting them, wrapping them in linen, and burying them in the sterile sand of the desert. The dry heat of the sun kept the bodies from decaying, even after several thousand years. By Hatshepsut's time, however, the Egyptians were embalming bodies in a more elaborate manner.

First, the embalmers opened the body and took out its inner organs. They washed the organs in palm wine, smeared them with oil, and wrapped them in linen. Then they placed most of the organs in four alabaster jars—one each for the liver, the stomach, the intestines, and the lungs. If these organs had remained in the body, it would have rotted. The heart and the brain were kept separate.

Next, the embalmers packed the body in natron to dry it out. When it was completely dry, the embalmers put back the heart, filled the skull with natron and plaster, and set obsidian eyes into the sockets. Then they wrapped the body very tightly in hundreds of yards of linen strips. The wrapped body, together with the dried brain, was placed in a wooden coffin on which was painted a portrait of the dead person. The coffin also contained rolls of verses from *The Book of the Dead*, as well as magic amulets. The coffin was then placed inside a second coffin, which was buried along with the four jars containing the body's liver, stomach, intestines, and lungs.

A body preserved in this manner is known as a *mummy*. The word mummy comes from the Arabic word *mumiyah*, meaning "pitch," which is a black sticky tree sap. When the Arabs (who conquered Egypt in 641 C.E.) first discovered mummies, they found that the oil inside many of the coffins had turned black, thus resembling pitch. The Arabs believed the mummies had magic powers and ground them up for use as medicine.

Modern scientists often use CAT scans to examine a mummy without opening its coffin.

A mummy of a cat, intricately wrapped in linen strips

In addition to human beings, the ancient Egyptians sometimes mummified animals, especially cats. In the mid-1800s C.E., a cemetery at the town of Beni-Hassan was found to contain about 300,000 mummified cats. Instead of being studied, however, the cat mummies were taken to England, where they were sold to farmers as fertilizer at a price of twenty-one dollars per ton.

A Multitude of Gods

Ancient Egyptian religion was filled with gods and goddesses. At first the inhabitants of each town worshipped a totem animal, such as a lion or a hippopotamus. The totem animals supposedly protected the people against danger. After a while, the gods and goddesses assumed human form with some animal characteristics. For example, Thoth, the god of wisdom and of scribes, had the head of an ibis because that bird appears wise as it stands motionless in the Nile. Horus, the god of the rising sun, bore the head of a falcon, a bird that soars high into the sky.

The most important Egyptian god was Amen-Re. He was a combination of two gods: Amen, the god of Thebes, and Re, the sun god from whom all pharaohs were supposedly descended. Over the centuries, the priests of Amen-Re received so many gifts of land, cattle, and other goods from the Egyptian people that they controlled about half of the country's wealth.

Another important god was Osiris, lord of the Underworld. According to legend, he was a former pharaoh. One day his evil brother Set killed him. Osiris's widow Isis found her husband's body, embalmed it, and placed it in a tomb. Then she and her young son Horus fled for safety to the marshes of the delta. When Horus grew up, he fought his wicked uncle Set and won. Although he lost an eye in the battle, it was restored to him by the god Thoth. Horus then went to his father's tomb, where he

offered to sacrifice his eye in exchange for Osiris's resurrection. Horus's offer was accepted, and Osiris rose from the dead. Later, he descended to the Underworld, "where he saw that justice and good continued to triumph over evil."

Osiris is pictured holding a crook, or shepherd's stick, in his right hand and a flail, an instrument for threshing grain, in his left. Pharaohs were often portrayed in a similar pose.

The Egyptians

PART THREE

An Egyptian tomb painting shows two views of the same noble family fishing and fowling along the banks of the Nile.

in Their Own Words

Archaeologists have unearthed thousands of letters written by the people of ancient Egypt. Then, as now, youngsters who had been sent away to school often complained when writing home:

Look here, this is my fifth letter to you, and you haven't written to me except once . . . and haven't come here. After assuring me, "I'm coming," you didn't come to find out whether my teacher was paying attention to me or not. And he asks about you practically every day. "Isn't he coming yet?" And I just say, "Yes." Do your best to come to me quickly, so he'll teach me as he's eager to do.

Apparently, the schoolboy's tuition had not yet been paid, and the teacher was unwilling to teach until he received the promised payment.

Wives, too, often complained to husbands who were absent abroad. One such letter was sent to a man who had temporarily entered a temple at Memphis and persisted in remaining there:

When I received your letter . . . in which you announce that you have become a recluse in Serapis's temple at Memphis, I immediately thanked the gods at hearing you were well, but your not coming home when all the other recluses have come home, I do not like one bit, because, after having piloted myself and your child through such a bad time and gone to every extremity because of the price of food, I thought that now, at least, with you home, I would get some respite, but you haven't even thought of coming home, haven't given any regard to our circumstances, how I was without everything even while you were here, to say nothing of so long a period passing and such bad times and your not having sent us anything.

What's more, Horus, who delivered your letter, reports that you've already gotten your release, so I really don't like it at all!

The reference to the man Horus indicates the main problem of writing letters in ancient Egypt, namely, how to get mail delivered. There was no public postal service, nor were there any private services. As a result, a letter writer had to find someone who was traveling to the city where the letter was being sent. Even then, making the actual delivery was difficult. Houses did not have numbers, and only the main streets of cities had names. One Egyptian letter carrier received the following delivery instructions:

> *From Moon Gate, walk as if toward the granaries . . . and at the first street back of the baths turn left. . . . Then go west. Then go down the steps and up the other steps and turn right. After the temple precinct there is a seven-[room] house with a basket-weaving establishment. Inquire there. . . . Then give a shout.*

In addition to letters, the ancient Egyptians wrote love poems, of which the following is an example:

> *I think I'll go home and lie very still,*
> *feigning terminal illness.*
> *Then the neighbors will all troop over to stare,*
> *my love, perhaps among them.*
> *How she'll smile while the specialists*
> *snarl in their teeth!—*
> *she perfectly well knows what ails me.*

The ancient Egyptians wrote numerous stories as well as poems. Some stories were tales of adventure. Others dealt with ideas, such

Besides listening to stories, ancient Egyptians enjoyed listening to music. The harp and the lute were probably their favorite instruments.

as whether it was possible to avoid one's destiny. Since most Egyptians could not read, storytellers recited the tales either in local taverns or in the homes of the rich. Two of the most popular tales of ancient Egypt are the following:

The Tale of a Shipwrecked Sailor

Let me tell you of what happened to me once. I was going to the mines of Pharaoh and I took a ship that was 225 feet in length and 60 feet in width and was manned by 150 of the best sailors in Egypt. They predicted that there would be little or no wind, but while we were still at sea a storm overtook us and the waves were twelve feet high. The ship went down and most of the crew perished. As I swam in the sea a plank drifted toward me and I lay on that. The sea bore me along and cast me upon an island. I spent three days alone hiding in a thicket. Then I became hungry and began to look around. I found figs and grapes, fruit, grain, and melons. Nothing was lacking, for it was a paradise. I dug a hole in the ground and prepared a burnt offering for the gods.

Suddenly I heard a loud noise like thunder. I thought it might be caused by a wave of the sea. The trees shook, the earth quaked, and I was afraid. I uncovered my face and found that the sound was caused by a gigantic serpent that was coming toward me. He was forty-five feet long; his body was overlaid with gold and his eyes were blue. He coiled himself up before me.

Then he opened his mouth as I lay on my face and he said to me, "What has brought you here, little one? Who has brought you to this island? If you delay in telling me I shall cause you to vanish." He took me in his mouth and carried me to his cave and put me down without any hurt. Here the [serpent] repeated his question: "Who brought you to this island which is in the sea?"

Then I humbled myself before him and replied, "I was embarked for the mines by order of the Pharaoh. A storm came upon us and I was carried to these shores on a plank."

The [serpent] answered, "Have no fear, little one, and do not be sad. It is the gods who have let you live and brought you to this isle of the blessed where nothing is lacking, for it is filled with good things. You will stay with me four months. Then a ship will come from your own country and you will return to Egypt and die in your own city. [Egyptians wanted to die in their hometown.] I too have passed through evil fortunes. There were seventy-five of us here until a fire destroyed everyone, but I survived. But be of good cheer; you will live to embrace your wife and children and live once again in your house. . . ."

A ship arrived in due time, as he had foretold. I climbed a tall tree to see who might be on it. When I reported to him I found that he already knew about it. "Farewell," the [serpent] said, "a safe journey home. You will see your family once again. May my name be well received in your city."

I bowed myself before him and he gave me precious gifts of perfumes, cassia, sweet woods, kohl, incense, ivory tusks, baboons, and apes. All these things I loaded on the ship. Then the [serpent] spoke once more to me. "You will arrive in your country in two months. You will embrace your children and be buried in your own tomb." I went to the shore and called the crew to me and we thanked the master of the island for his kindness.

We reached the [royal] Residence in two months as the [serpent] had predicted. I presented the gifts from the island to the sovereign, who thanked me in the presence of all the nobles and appointed me to be one of his bodyguards.

So you see . . . I have seen much and have attained success in spite of my misfortunes. Give heed to what I have said, for it is wise to listen.

The Tale of the Doomed Prince

There was once a king who had no son. He prayed to the gods that he might have an heir and they said his prayer would be answered. When the young prince was born, the Seven Hathors came to decree his fate. They said, "He shall die by the crocodile, the snake, or the dog."

Naturally the king was very sad at hearing this. He ordered a stone house to be built and shut the prince up in it, along with every thing he could possibly want. But when the prince was older, he went up on the roof one day and saw a man walking along the road with a dog beside him; and he asked that a dog be procured for him. His father, who yearned to please the poor lad, caused a puppy to be given him.

After the prince was grown he demanded his release, saying, "If it is my doom it will come to me, whatever I do." Sadly his father agreed; and the boy set forth, accompanied by his dog. At last he came to the kingdom of Naharin [Syria]. The king had only one child, a daughter; and he had placed her in a tower whose window was seventy cubits from the ground, and told all the princes who wanted to marry her that she would be given to the one who first reached her window.

Disguised as a chariot driver, the Prince of Egypt joined the young men who spent all their days jumping up at the window of the princess; and the princess saw him. When finally he reached the window she kissed and embraced him. But when the King of Naharin heard that a common chariot driver had won his daughter, he tried first to send the boy away and then to kill him. But the princess clasped the young man in her arms and said, "I will not stay alive an hour longer than he!"

So the lovers were wed; and after some time had elapsed, the prince told his wife about the three fates. "Have the dog that follows you killed!" she exclaimed; but he replied, "I will not allow my dog, which I raised from a puppy, to be killed." So she guarded him day and night.

One day the prince decided he wanted to go back to Egypt on a visit. His wife feared for his safety, so she insisted on going along. They came to a town situated on a river and found a place in which to stay. When night came, the prince lay down on his couch and fell asleep. His wife set out jars of beer and wine by his side, and she waited. Suddenly a snake came out of its hole to bite the prince. But it drank the wine and became drunk, and rolled over on its back; and the wife took her ax and chopped it to pieces.

The prince awoke and his wife said, "See, you have been delivered from one of your fates. Surely you will be saved from the others."

A few days later the prince took a walk with his dog. While chasing wild game, the dog plunged into the river. The prince followed him. Out came a crocodile, who seized the prince and carried him off. As he bore him along, the crocodile said to the prince, "I am your fate and I have been pursuing you and . . ."

(This tale is incomplete because the papyrus on which it was written breaks off before the end.)

Ptah-hotep was a minister of state who lived in Egypt about 750 years before Hatshepsut. Near the end of his life, he drew up a list of rules that he urged his son to follow in order to live wisely and happily. The rules show what people of that time considered to be moral values. Among the things Ptah-hotep said to his son were the following:

> • *Be not proud because of your learning. Listen to the uneducated as well as the educated. If you desire to act worthily, stay away from evil and beware of greed.*
> • *Try to be cheerful as long as you live.*
> • *If you are in a position of responsibility, listen to the requests of [the petitioner]. Do not judge him until you have heard all that he has to say. It is an ornament of the heart to listen kindly.*
> • *Although misfortune may occur to carry away wealth, the power of righteousness is that it endures. A man who lives by doing right . . . shall endure forever.*

The ancient Egyptians believed that dreams foretold the future, and they recorded the meaning of dream symbols in special dream books. The following list of symbols is taken from a dream book written in Thebes about 150 years after Hatshepsut's death. If people's dreams were bad, they recited a series of magic spells as soon as they awoke in hopes that the spells would change their future and turn evil fortune away:

If a Man Sees Himself in a Dream:

with a bow in his hand,	*good:* a great office will be given to him.
seeing a serpent,	*good:* this means food.
sight-seeing in the city of Osiris,	*good:* he will have a great old age.
plunging into the river,	*good:* he will be cleansed of all evils.
drinking warm beer,	*bad:* suffering will come upon him.
seeing a dwarf,	*bad:* it means taking away of half of his life.
seeing people far off,	*bad:* his death is near.

The eye of Horus can be seen in two places in this painting from *The Book of the Dead*. Egyptian astronomers associated Horus with the planet Mars, which they called Horus the Red because of its reddish appearance.

Tuthmosis III led his troops into battle almost every year for twenty years. The accounts of his military campaigns were carved on the walls of one of the great temples he had built. The following selections list some of the spoils from his first and fifth campaigns:

> *340 living prisoners; 83 hands; 2,041 mares; 191 foals; 6 stallions; . . . a beautiful chariot, wrought with gold, belonging to the chief of Megiddo; . . . 892 chariots of his wretched army; . . . 200 suits of armor, belonging to his wretched army; 502 bows; 7 poles of wood, wrought with silver, belonging to the tent of that foe. Behold, the army of his majesty took 1,929 large cattle, 2,000 small [goats], 20,500 white small [sheep].*
>
>   *List of the tribute brought to his majesty on this expedition: 51 slaves, male and female; 30 horses; 10 flat dishes of silver; incense oil, 470 jars of honey, 6,428 jars of wine, copper, lead, lapis lazuli, green feldspar. . . . All good fruit of this country. Behold, the army of his majesty was drunk and anointed with oil every day as at a feast in Egypt.*

Among the Eighteenth Dynasty successors of Tuthmosis III was Amenhotep IV, a believer in the cult of Aton. This cult held that Egypt's many gods were really aspects of a single god named Aton, whose symbol was the sun disk. Amenhotep IV—who changed his name to Akhenaton, or "he who serves Aton"—wrote a magnificent hymn to his god:

Glorious is your splendor rising o'er the far horizon,
O vibrant, vital Aton! You are the source of all life.
When you appear over the eastern heavens,
O, you flood all the earth with your beauty!
How radiant, how mighty, when high above
You embrace the lands of all your creation!
You are the Sun! You glow o'er all in your universal love.
Far distant, yet the world receives you.
Though you are in the heavens, yet the day follows in
your path.
The great ships glide up and down the rivers;
All highways fly open at your coming.
The very fishes in the streams leap upward toward you;
You gleam down upon the mighty seas.

.   .   .   .

Oh, you dwell in my soul, O Sun!

.   .   .   .

You make me wise in your ways;
You grant me your strength.
All things of this world are in your hand;
They are as you have created them.
When you rise, all live;
When you go down, all is death.

The pharaoh Akhenaton main-
tained an aviary and a wild animal
enclosure at his northern palace.
He was happily married to
Nefertiti, one of ancient Egypt's
most beautiful women.

Glossary

The Book of the Dead: A scroll of magic spells that was supposed to help dead Egyptians pass into the Underworld safely.

dynasty: A series of rulers from the same family.

lapis lazuli: A blue gemstone.

mortuary temple: A temple devoted to a dead pharaoh; it sometimes contained the ruler's tomb.

natron: A mineral made up of sodium carbonate and bicarbonate that is used for washing.

obsidian: A black stone formed by the rapid cooling of lava; used to make sharp knives and also jewelry.

precedent: An action or decision that may serve as an example to be followed in the future.

queen consort: The wife of a reigning king.

recluse: A person who withdraws from everyday life and lives either all alone or in a religious institution with other recluses.

regent: The person who governs a kingdom during the period when the rightful ruler is too young to take command.

salve: A soothing cream or ointment.

satire: A writing that pokes fun at foolish situations or people.

scribe: A writer.

terrace: A raised bank of earth with a flat top and sloping sides; a terraced area looks somewhat like a broad series of steps.

totem: A special animal that symbolizes a group such as a tribe or the inhabitants of a particular region.

tunic: A loose-fitting garment, either sleeved or sleeveless.

For Further Reading

Aldred, Cyril. *The Egyptians.* London: Thomas & Hudson, 1984.

Crosher, Judith. *Ancient Egypt.* New York: Viking, 1992.

Janssen, Rosemary M. and Jac J. *Growing Up in Ancient Egypt.* London: Rubicon Press, 1990.

Johnston, Darcie C. *Egypt: Land of the Pharaohs.* Alexandria, VA: Time-Life Books, 1992.

Marston, Elsa. *The Ancient Egyptians.* Cultures of the Past Series. New York: Marshall Cavendish, 1996.

Price, Christine. *Made in Ancient Egypt.* New York: E. P. Dutton & Co., 1970.

Smith, Brenda. *Egypt of the Pharaohs.* San Diego: Lucent Books, 1996.

Bibliography

Bratton, Fred G. *Myths and Legends of the Ancient Near East.* New York: Thomas Y. Crowell Company, 1970.

Breasted, James Henry. *Ancient Records of Egypt.* Chicago: University of Chicago Press, 1906.

Casson, Lionel. "It Would Be Very Nice If You Sent Me 200 Drachmas." *Smithsonian,* April 1983, pp. 116–131.

Collier, Joy. *The Heretic Pharaoh.* New York: Dorset Press, 1994.

Fairservis, Walter A., Jr. *Egypt, Gift of the Nile.* New York: Macmillan Company, 1963.

Foster, John L. *Love Songs of the New Kingdom.* New York: Charles Scribner's Sons, 1974.

Grimal, Nicolas. *A History of Ancient Egypt.* Cambridge, MA: Blackwell, 1992.

Holland, Barbara. *Secrets of the Cat.* New York: Ballantine Books, 1988.

Holliday, Carl. *The Dawn of Literature.* New York: Frederick Ungar Publishing Co., 1962.

James, T. G. H. *Pharaoh's People.* London: Bodley Head, 1984.

Kaster, Joseph, trans. and ed. *Wings of the Falcon.* New York: Holt, Rinehart and Winston, 1968.

Lichtheim, Miriam. *Ancient Egyptian Literature.* Vols. 1 and 2. Berkeley: University of California Press, 1973–1976.

Mertz, Barbara. *Temples, Tombs and Hieroglyphs.* New York: Coward-McCann, 1964.

Peters, Elizabeth. *The Snake, the Crocodile & the Dog.* New York: Warner Books, 1992.

Pritchard, James B., ed. *Ancient Near Eastern Texts.* Princeton, NJ: Princeton University Press, 1950.

Sewell, Barbara. *Egypt under the Pharaohs.* New York: G. P. Putnam's Sons, 1968.

Stead, Miriam. *Egyptian Life.* Cambridge, MA: Harvard University Press, 1986.

Tyldesley, Joyce. *Daughters of Isis.* New York: Penguin Books, 1995.

———. *Hatshepsut: The Female Pharaoh.* New York: Viking, 1996.

White, Jon Manchip. *Everyday Life in Ancient Egypt.* New York: G. P. Putnam's Sons, 1963.

Winer, Bart. *Life in the Ancient World.* New York: Random House, 1961.

ON-LINE INFORMATION*

http:/www.julen.net/ancient/index.html
> This collection of links can be searched for information on the time of Hatshepsut.

http://www.dalmatia.net/lupic/egypt/index.htm
> Excellent resource for exploring ancient Egypt and other countries of the ancient world.

http://www.omnibusol.com/ancient.html#Section 5

*Websites change from time to time. For additional on-line information, check with the media specialist at your local library.

A Note on Names and Dates

Did you notice how often the words *probably, apparently, perhaps,* and *about* appear in this book? There are reasons why scholars are not certain about the exact dates of many events in ancient Egypt's history. For one thing, each time a new pharaoh came to the throne, the Egyptians began counting from the year 1 again. The only way to keep track of historical events is through long lists of rulers. But the lists do not always agree. So the dates for Hatshepsut's reign, for example, range from 1504–1482 B.C.E. to 1479–1457 B.C.E.

Sometimes there is not enough evidence for a definite statement and instead, scholars make a reasonable assumption. For example, there is no recorded date as to when Tuthmosis III became pharaoh with Hatshepsut as regent. But his mummy is that of a middle-aged man rather than an old one, and we know he reigned for more than fifty years. So he must have come to the throne when he was five years or younger, not a teenager.

Another source of bewilderment is the different ways of spelling names. Each pharaoh has at least two names, one Egyptian and the other a Greek form. Thus, Thutmose I and Tuthmosis I are the same person. In addition, scholars spell Egyptian names in different ways. That is because hieroglyphs do not include vowels and the correct pronunciation is an educated guess. Accordingly, Hatshepsut is also referred to as Hatchepsut, Hatshopsitu, Hatshepsowe, and Hatshepsuit. This book uses the most familiar forms of names.

Likewise, although the archaeological evidence allows for a variety of interpretations, this book's account of Hatshepsut's life is the one most widely accepted by historians. If additional evidence is discovered in the future, it may be that Hatshepsut's life story will once again be revised.

Notes

Part One: Lady of the Two Lands

p. 9 "The pool of the hippopotami": Mertz, *Temples, Tombs and Hieroglyphs*, p. 153.

p. 9 "from the Horns of the Earth": Mertz, *Temples, Tombs and Hieroglyphs*, p. 161.

p. 19 "his life's work": Tyldesley, *Hatshepsut*, p. 144.

p. 21 "wounded male pride": Tyldesley, *Hatshepsut*, p. 226.

Part Two: Everyday Life in Hatshepsut's Egypt

p. 32 "stank more than fish roe": Pritchard, *Ancient Near Eastern Texts*, p. 433.

p. 36 "Keep thy tongue": Collier, *The Heretic Pharaoh*, p. 82.

p. 36 "Don't accept the gift": Lichtheim, *Ancient Egyptian Literature*, vol. 2, p. 158.

p. 36 "Wait quietly": Kaster, *Wings of the Falcon*, p. 169.

p. 37 "The ear of a lad": James, *Pharaoh's People*, p. 141.

p. 43 "love your wife": Lichtheim, *Ancient Egyptian Literature*, vol. 1, p. 69.

p. 51 "Spend a happy day": White, *Everyday Life in Ancient Egypt*, p. 189.

p. 52 "I have not committed evil": Winer, *Life in the Ancient World*, p. 63.

p. 52 "bread to the hungry": Winer, *Life in the Ancient World*, p. 63.

p. 59 "where he saw that justice": Fairservis, *Egypt, Gift of the Nile*, p. 113.

Part Three: The Egyptians in Their Own Words

p. 62 "Look here, this is my fifth letter": Casson, "It Would Be Very Nice If You Sent Me 200 Drachmas," pp. 122, 124.

p. 63 "When I received your letter": Casson, "It Would Be Very Nice If You Sent Me 200 Drachmas," p. 131.

p. 64 "From Moon Gate": Casson, "It Would Be Very Nice If You Sent Me 200 Drachmas," p. 120.

p. 64 "I think I'll go home": Foster, *Love Songs of the New Kingdom*, p. 72.

p. 66 "Let me tell you": Bratton, *Myths and Legends of the Ancient Near East*, pp. 81–84.

p. 68 "There was once a king": Peters, *The Snake, the Crocodile & the Dog*, pp. 51–52 and Bratton, *Myths and Legends of the Ancient Near East*, pp. 91, 94.

p. 70 "Be not proud": Fairservis, *Egypt, Gift of the Nile*, p. 61.

p. 71 "If a Man Sees Himself": Kaster, *Wings of the Falcon*, pp. 193–194.

p. 72 "340 living prisoners": Breasted, *Ancient Records of Egypt*, pp. 187–188.

p. 73 "Glorious is your splendor": based on Holliday, *The Dawn of Literature*, pp. 41–42.

Index

Page numbers for illustrations are in boldface.